NATURAL IS BEAUTIFUL

NATURAL IS POWERFUL

"Hi Soriya, I've been looking everywhere for you!"
"Hi Kosal, why do you look so excited?" asks Soriya.
"Have you seen the new girl in our class?"
"She has something very strange on her head,"
Remarks Kosal excitedly.
"I wonder what it is," Soriya contemplates.
"I'm going to find out," Kosal Announces.

"Hello! My name is Kosal. What's your name?"
"Hello, my name is Mto."
"Where are you from?" Kosal inquires.
"I'm from Kenya," says Mto.
"I'm from Cambodia," Says Kosal excitedly.

"What's that on your head?" Kosal inquires.
"This is my hair," replies Mto,
with a puzzled look on her face.
"That's not hair," retorts Kosal.
"Yes it is!" responds Mto.
"It is very big and round," says Kosal.

"Can I touch it?" asks Kosal.

"Okay," Mto reluctantly obliges.

Kosal cautiously extends his little hand

and touches Mto's soft, tight curls.

"Woooow," he says in amazement. He thinks for a

moment then loudly exclaims, "I still don't believe you!

My hair is straight, why is yours not straight?"

"Because I'm African and our hair is

curly and springy!" says Mto.

"Your hair is lying!" yells Kosal.

"Papa, is my hair lying?"

"What do you mean, my sweet pea?" Papa asks.

"Kosal said my hair is lying," explains Mto with a sad face.

"Who is Kosal?"

"A boy with straight hair at my new school," says Mto.

"Why did he say your hair was lying?"

"Because my hair is big and round and curly and springy! Not straight like his hair."

"Oh my darling, your hair is not lying.
Children from different races are born with
different kinds of hair.
I think Kosal has never seen an afro before, And
thinks any hair that is not straight is fake hair."

There is wavy hair!

THERE IS CURLY HAIR!

There is straight hair!

There is spikey hair!

AND OF COURSE! THERE IS BOUNCY, SPRINGY CURLS LIKE MY MTO'S!

"YOU KNOW SOMETHING ELSE?" ASKS PAPA.

"WHAT?" ASKS MTO IN ANTICIPATION.

"THERE ARE DIFFERENT COLORS OF HAIR TOO!"

"REALLY, PAPA?"

"YES," REPLIES PAPA.

There is black hair!

THERE IS BROWN HAIR!

AND BLONDE HAIR!

RED HAIR TOO!

"Papa! Which hair is the most beautiful?"
"Oh my darling girl, none is more beautiful than the other.
They are all equally beautiful."
"Is my hair beautiful too, Papa?"
"Of course my love, yours is as beautiful as Kosal's
hair and all the rest."
"And my hair is noy lying?" asks Mto.
"No sweet pea, Your hair is not lying.
Your afro is true!
Just the way it is!"

All hair is true and beautiful!

www.ingramcontent.com/pod-product-compliance
Lightning Source LLC
Chambersburg PA
CBHW041442290326

41933CB00034B/46